DATE DUE

ANCIENT GREEKS

DRESS, EAT, WRITE, AND PLAY JUST LIKE THE GREEKS

JOE FULLMAN

QEB Publishing

Copyright © QEB Publishing, Inc. 2009

Published in the United States by
QEB Publishing, Inc.
3 Wrigley, Suite A
Irvine, CA 92618
www.qeb-publishing.com

Library of Congress Cataloging-in-Publication Data

Fullman, Joe.
  Ancient Greeks : dress, eat, write, and play just like the Greeks /
Joe Fullman.
     p. cm. -- (QEB hands-on history)
  Includes index.
  ISBN 978-1-59566-152-4 (hardcover)
  1. Greece--History--Juvenile literature. I. Title.
  DF215.F856 2010
  938--dc22

                              200900111

Printed and bound in China

Author Joe Fullman
Consultant John Malam
Project Editor Ben Hubbard
Designer Lisa Peacock
Project Maker Veronica Lenz

Publisher Steve Evans
Creative Director Zeta Davies
Managing Editor Amanda Askew

Picture credits
(t=top, b=bottom, l=left, r=right, c=center, fc=front cover)

Alamy Images 6b Jason Wood, 8t Mary Evans Picture
Library, 14b The London Art Archive, 20t Ace Stock Ltd,
24t The London Art Archive, 26t The Print Collector

Bridgeman Art Library 18b Private Collection/Look
and Learn, 28t Private Collection/Archives Charmet

Corbis 5tl Christie's Images, 16t Hoberman Collection,
23t The Picture Desk/Gianni Dagli Orti, 29t Bettmann/
Corbis

Dreamstime 6t Wiltding, 8bl Phillip Gray

Fotolibra fc Chris James

Getty Images 4b The Bridgeman Art Library,
18t The Bridgeman Art Library, 20b Franck Fife/AFP,
22bl Hulton Archive/ General Photographic Agency

Photolibrary 10b Michael Runkel, 15tl Age Fotostock/
Wojtek Buss, 16b Imagestate/Steve Vidler, 19tl Index
Stock Imagery, 22t Imagebroker.net/Christian Handl
4t Krechet, 12t Elpis Ioannidis 24b Kharlanov Evgeny, 24c
Paul Cowan, 27bl AriyEvgeny, 24c Paul Cowan, 27bl Ariy

Simon Pask 5tc, 5 tr, 5cl, 5cr, 5bl, 5br, 7tl,7tr, 7cl, 7cr, 7bl,
7br, 8cr, 8br, 9tr, 9tl, 9br, 9bl, 11tr, 11tl, 11cr, 11cl, 11bl, 11br,
12bl, 12br, 13cl, 13cr, 13bl, 13br, 15tr, 15cl, 15cr, 15bl, 15br,
17tr, 17cl, 17cr, 17bl, 17br, 19tr, 19tc, 19cl, 19cr, 19bl, 19br,
21tr, 21tl, 21cl, 21cr, 21bl, 21br, 22c, 22br, 23cl, 23cr, 23bl,
23br, 25tr, 25tl, 25cl, 25cr, 25bl, 25br, 27tr, 27tl, 27cl, 27cr,
27br, 28b, 29cl, 29cr, 29bl, 29br

Topham Picturepoint 20t Ann Ronan Picture Library/
HIP, 13t Alinari, 14t The Print Collector/HIP, 17tl, Charles
Walker, 26b

TAKE CARE
WHEN USING SCISSORS

Words in **bold** are
explained in the glossary
on page 30.

CONTENTS

WHO WERE THE ANCIENT GREEKS?

The ancient Greeks lived in a country called Greece, thousands of years ago. Ancient Greece was not a single **empire** with one ruler. Instead it was a group of separate **states**, which shared the same culture and language. Over time, the ancient Greeks also set up **colonies** in many other places, including Italy, Spain, France, Turkey, and North Africa.

The ancient Greek empire was made up of a group of separate states, including Athens. ▶

This temple to the Greek god Apollo, in Didyma, Turkey, was one of the largest buildings in the ancient Greek world. ▼

A ROMAN PROVINCE

The ancient Greeks were defeated by the Romans in 146 BC. Greece then became part of the Roman world. However, the Greek way of life didn't die out. The Romans liked Greek culture. They copied their buildings and the way they dressed. They even **worshipped** many of the same gods, although they gave them new Roman names.

A GREAT CIVILIZATION

Ancient Greece was home to many great **philosophers**, artists, writers, scientists, and mathematicians. Their ideas were still studied after the Greek civilization came to an end. In fact, books by ancient Greek writers, such as Socrates and Plato, are still read today.

A sculpture of the famous Greek philosopher, Plato. ▶

DID YOU KNOW?
THE ANCIENT GREEKS WERE SKILLED POTTERS. MANY VASES FROM ANCIENT GREECE HAVE BEEN FOUND. SOME ARE MORE THAN 3,000 YEARS OLD.

This black and orange vase was made in the 6th century BC.

MAKE A GREEK STORY VASE

The ancient Greeks decorated "story vases" with pictures of gods, heroes and monsters.

1

Blow up the balloon. Apply two layers of newspaper strips and glue to the balloon. Leave to dry.

2

Repeat until you have eight layers. When the vase is dry, pop the balloon with a pin.

3

Cut 4 strips of cardstock. Tape one each around the base and top, and one on either side to make handles.

4

Glue three layers of newspaper strips to the base, top, and sides. Make the strips overlap.

5

When dry, paint the vase red and the base, rim, and handles black. Decorate with a design and leave to dry.

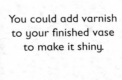

You could add varnish to your finished vase to make it shiny.

5

THE EARLY GREEKS

The first **civilization** in the Greek world was set up on the island of Crete, about 6,000 years ago. The people here grew olives, grapes, and grain. Over time, they became rich by **trading** with other peoples from Europe and Africa. They lived in large settlements, at the heart of which was a palace. The biggest palace was at Knossos. The **archeologist** who found it thought it had been built by King Minos. He named the people Minoans, after this legendary king.

The ruins of the palace at Knossos on Crete. The red pillars were built to show what the palace used to look like.

THE MYCENAEANS

In about 1450 BC, a volcanic eruption close to Crete ended the Minoan civilization. After this, the Mycenaeans, from mainland Greece, became the most powerful people in the Greek world. One of their main settlements was at Mycenae. However, by about 1200 BC the Mycenaean civilization had also faded away.

THE MINOTAUR

The Greeks told stories about a monster on Crete called the Minotaur, who was half man and half bull. He lived in a labyrinth—a difficult maze that no one could escape from. Eventually, a Greek hero called Theseus entered the labyrinth and killed the Minotaur. He then used a length of string that he had tied to the entrance to find his way out again.

DID YOU KNOW?
BETWEEN 1200 AND 800 BC, GREEK SETTLEMENTS WERE LESS SUCCESSFUL THAN BEFORE. NOT MUCH IS KNOWN ABOUT THE GREEKS DURING THIS TIME, WHICH IS WHY IT IS CALLED THE "DARK AGES."

The Minotaur had a human's body and a bull's head.

MAKE A MINOTAUR MASK

The Minotaur was often shown in Greek art.

◄ Tie the string around the back of your head—you're now the Minotaur!

YOU WILL NEED
PLAIN CARDSTOCK • GOLD CARDSTOCK • PENCIL • SCISSORS • PAINTBRUSH AND PAINTS • HOLE PUNCH • TWO PIECES OF STRING, 12 IN (30 CM) LONG • STAPLER

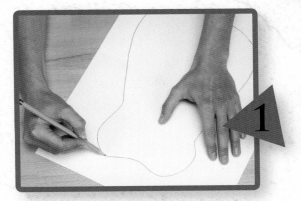

Draw the shape of the bull's face onto the cardstock. Be sure to make it bigger than your own face.

Sketch the Minotaur's features, then paint the whole face. Cut out around the mask.

Draw two horns onto the gold cardstock. Cut them out. Staple both of the horns to the mask.

Mark the eyeholes and punch them out using the hole punch.

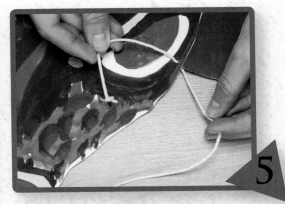

Make two small holes either side of the mask. Thread string through each hole and tie a knot.

THE TROJAN WAR

Greek legends tell of a war fought in about 1300 BC between Greeks from Mycenae and Trojans from the city of Troy, in Turkey. A poem called the *Iliad*, written by the Greek poet Homer, tells us what happened in the war. Homer describes gods, heroes, and monsters, which are probably made up. However, historians believe that a war between the Greeks and the Trojans did happen.

▲ Greek and Trojan soldiers fought fiercely during the Trojan War.

MAKE A TROJAN HORSE

The ancient Greeks built their horse on wheels, so the Trojans could bring it inside the city gates.

YOU WILL NEED

SMALL COOKIE BOX • PENCIL
5 CARDBOARD TUBES • RULER
CARDSTOCK • SCISSORS
WHITE SCHOOL GLUE
PAINTBRUSH AND PAINTS
STICKY TAPE • MARKER PEN

◀ This modern replica of the wooden horse stands outside the entrance to the ruins of Troy.

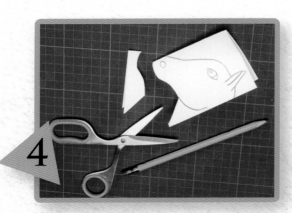

1

Use sticky tape to stick the lid of your cookie box down. Cut a door in the side to put things inside.

4

Fold a piece of cardstock in half. Draw the horse's head, with the horse's nose touching the fold. Cut out.

8

THE WOODEN HORSE

According to the legend, the war lasted more than ten years. The Greeks surrounded the city of Troy, but could not get inside it. Instead, they pretended to go home, but left behind a large wooden horse as a gift for the Trojans. Thinking the war was over, the Trojans brought the horse inside the city. However, they didn't realize that Greek soldiers were hidden inside the horse. The Greeks jumped out and captured the city.

DID YOU KNOW?
IN THE *ILIAD*, THE TROJAN WAR STARTED BECAUSE PARIS, THE PRINCE OF TROY, STOLE HELEN, THE WIFE OF THE KING OF SPARTA. HELEN WAS THOUGHT TO BE THE MOST BEAUTIFUL WOMAN IN THE WORLD.

THE REAL TROY

After Troy was destroyed, people left and it became covered over with earth. For a long time no one knew where it was. However, in the 19th century, a German archeologist called Heinrich Schliemann rediscovered the remains of a city, which he believed was Troy, in northern Turkey.

Cut a small section from the top of each of your five cardboard tubes.

Glue four tubes to the bottom of your box for the legs and the other to the top of the box for a neck.

You could store things such as coins inside your wooden horse.

Glue the head to the neck. Paint the horse brown and draw the planks of wood with marker pen.

9

THE GREEK WORLD

From the 8th century BC onward, the Greeks became more powerful. They built large **settlements** on mainland Greece, including Athens, Sparta, and Corinth. These places are known as **city-states**, because each one had its own ruler and was free from the others. The Greeks also created new colonies overseas.

WARFARE
The city-states often went to war with each other. However, sometimes they joined together to fight an enemy, such as the **Persian Empire**. Greek soldiers wore helmets and body armor and carried shields. Their main weapons were swords and long wooden spears with sharp metal points. The Greeks also used catapults and battering rams.

▲

Greek soldiers were known as hoplites. Their helmets had decorative plumes on top.

ALEXANDER THE GREAT
Alexander became the leader of Macedonia, a kingdom in ancient Greece, in 336 BC. Soon after, he led an army of soldiers from all the city-states against the Persian Empire—the Greeks' most powerful enemy. He defeated the Persians and created a huge empire, stretching all the way from Greece to India.

DID YOU KNOW?
ALEXANDER CREATED MORE THAN 70 CITIES. HE NAMED MOST OF THEM AFTER HIMSELF, INCLUDING ALEXANDRIA IN EGYPT, WHICH STILL STANDS TODAY.

Founded by Alexander in 332 BC, Alexandria became one of the greatest cities in the ancient Greek world.

▼

MAKE A GREEK WAR HELMET

Greek soldiers wore bronze helmets with a bright plume—a decoration made from a strip of colored animal hair or feathers.

YOU WILL NEED
BALLOON • NEWSPAPER STRIPS
WHITE SCHOOL GLUE • PIN
SCISSORS • THIN CARDSTOCK,
12 IN (30 CM) BY 8 IN (20 CM)
PAINTBRUSH AND PAINTS
MARKER PEN • GLUE • RULER

1 Blow up the balloon a bit bigger than your head. Apply the newspaper strips and glue to ¾ of the balloon.

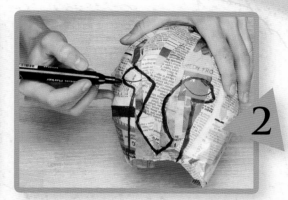

2 When dry, pop the balloon. Draw the eyeholes and nose guard onto the helmet. Carefully cut them out.

3 Fold the cardstock lengthwise. Then make another fold about 0.5 in (1.5 cm) from the first fold.

4 Cut 0.5 in (1.5 cm) strips all the way along the cardstock up to the second fold line. This will be the plume.

5 Paint the helmet and plume. When dry, attach the plume to the top of the helmet with glue.

Now your helmet is ready to wear. You could try making different kinds of plumes—with different colors or even with paper feathers.

ATHENS

B y the 5th century BC, Athens had become the largest and most important Greek city-state. Today, it is still Greece's largest city. The first settlers built their homes on top of a hill for defense. This settlement was known as the Acropolis (which means "hill city") and it was surrounded by a high wall. As the city grew and people felt safer, they began living on the land lower down. The homes at the top were replaced by **temples** and other buildings.

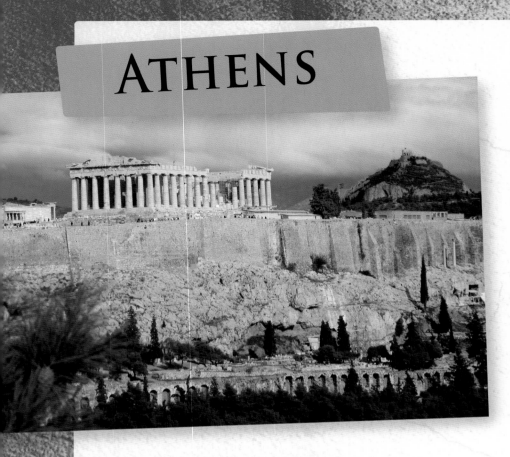

◀ The Parthenon was built 2,500 years ago. Even though it has been badly damaged, most of its columns are still standing.

PARTHENON

The largest and most important temple in Athens was the Parthenon. It was built on the highest point of the Acropolis. The temple was made for the goddess Athena—this is where Athens gets its name. It was built in the 5th century BC, and much of it still survives today.

MAKE A GREEK TEMPLE

The Greeks developed a style of temples that were built with columns and friezes. A frieze told a story in pictures.

YOU WILL NEED
10 CARDBOARD TUBES, 6 IN (15 CM) LONG • WHITE CARDSTOCK
SCISSORS • PENCIL • RULER • GLUE
PAINTBRUSH AND PAINTS
1 PIECE OF SMALL CARDSTOCK, 8 IN (21 CM) X 3 IN (8 CM) • 2 PIECES OF MEDIUM CARDSTOCK, 12 IN (30 CM) X 8 IN (20 CM) • 1 PIECE OF LARGE CARDSTOCK, 12 IN (30 CM) X 12 IN (30 CM)

1

Paint the cardboard tubes white.

2

Stick the columns to one piece of medium-sized cardstock. Stick the other piece of cardstock on top.

ATHENA

Athena was the daughter of the Greek god leader, Zeus. She was the goddess of warfare and wisdom, and is usually shown in statues wearing armor and carrying a shield and a spear. She is also shown with an owl, which was a symbol of wisdom.

◀ A huge gold and ivory statue of Athena used to stand inside the Parthenon.

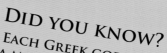
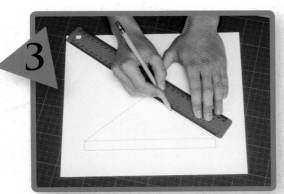

3

Mark out two triangles for your friezes on the small cardstock, with a 0.5 in (1.5 cm) border all around.

4

Paint your story onto the triangles and fold the border over on each side.

5

Stick the friezes to either end of the temple. Fold the large piece of cardstock into a roof. Glue on the top.

Most temples were light in color with friezes to tell stories about gods and goddesses. ▶

13

THE PEOPLE DECIDE

In the beginning, city-states were ruled by just a few rich landowners called **tyrants**. They lived in large houses decorated with **frescoes** and made all the decisions about the city. Most people were poor. They lived in small houses and worked in the fields. They had no say in how their city was run.

This modern painting shows what Athens' agora—or "meeting place"—might have looked like in ancient times.

DEMOCRACY
In Athens, the poor people became fed up with the rich people making all the decisions. In 508 BC, they threw out the tyrants and made a new sort of government called a **democracy**, which means "power of the people." Decisions about the city were made at large meetings, called assemblies, which any **free man** could go to.

Briseis, the wife of a Trojan king, was captured in battle and became a slave for the Greek warrior Achilles.

DID YOU KNOW?
SLAVES WEREN'T ALWAYS SLAVES FOREVER. SOMETIMES A SLAVE MIGHT EARN ENOUGH MONEY TO BUY BACK THEIR FREEDOM FROM THEIR MASTER.

SLAVERY
There were many **slaves** in Athens in ancient times. Slaves were often prisoners of war who had been captured in battle, or sometimes they were poor people who owed money that they could not pay back. Slaves did housework for rich people and worked in the fields and mines. They had no rights and could not vote.

MAKE A FRESCO

The homes of rich people were often decorated with a special type of picture called a fresco. Frescos are made by painting on wet plaster.

YOU WILL NEED
PLASTER OF PARIS • SPOON
MIXING BOWL • JUG OF WATER
SHOEBOX LID • PAINTBRUSH
AND PAINTS

Dolphin frescoes decorated the queen's wall at the palace of Knossos, Crete.

Use the lid of the shoebox as your frame. Cover the frame with black paint and leave it to dry.

Mix the plaster of Paris with water until the plaster is soft.

Pour the plaster into the frame. When the plaster starts to harden, paint a decorative frame.

You could hang your ancient Greek fresco on a wall or place it on a shelf.

Then paint the main picture of dolphins and fish.

Gods and Religion

The Greeks worshipped many different gods. They believed that the gods controlled everything. In Greek myth, the gods often behaved like humans – arguing, having fights, falling in love, and having children. The king of the gods, Zeus, was thought to rule over the other gods from his palace on Mount Olympus.

Zeus, the king of the Greek gods, was often shown on Greek coins. ▶

▲ There were two temples at Delphi—this small temple to Athena, which stood at the entrance, and a much larger temple to Apollo.

TEMPLES

The Greeks built large temples made out of stone for their gods. Here, the people would worship and give things to the gods, such as food, to keep them happy. The Greeks also sacrificed animals to their gods. The Greeks believed that if they pleased their gods, the gods would make sure they had enough food to eat and would help them win battles.

ORACLES

The Greeks wanted their gods to tell them about the future. In a town called Delphi, there was a temple to Apollo, the god of **prophecy**. Greek leaders would travel to Delphi to ask a priestess, known as the oracle, questions about the future. The priestess usually gave an unclear answer that could mean many different things.

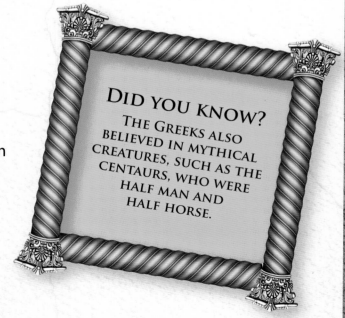

DID YOU KNOW?
THE GREEKS ALSO BELIEVED IN MYTHICAL CREATURES, SUCH AS THE CENTAURS, WHO WERE HALF MAN AND HALF HORSE.

This statue shows a griffin, a mythical creature with the body of a lion and the head and wings of an eagle.

◄

Color in your creature with colored pencils. You can make it as weird and wonderful as you like. ►

MAKE A MYTHICAL CREATURE

The Greeks told lots of stories about mythical creatures. These creatures were usually made up of parts of different animals.

YOU WILL NEED
PIECE OF PAPER • PENCIL
TWO FRIENDS • COLORED
PENCILS

1

Draw a creature's head at the top of the paper. Fold the paper and add two lines as a guide for the body.

2

Ask a friend to draw a body and arms. Then, fold the paper and draw two lines as a guide for the legs.

3

Ask your other friend to draw the legs.

4

Now open the paper to see your mythical creature.

17

FESTIVALS AND CULTURE

The Greeks held many **festivals** to celebrate their gods, with music and dancing. Many animals would be sacrificed, cooked, and eaten at a huge feast. Sporting contests were also held. Sports were very popular in ancient Greece. Boys played sports from an early age. They would learn how to wrestle, how to ride a chariot, and how to throw a javelin.

Carved in around 500 BC, this **relief** shows a group of Greek athletes playing a ball game.

FREE TIME

In rich people's homes, slaves did most of the hard work. This left the rich people with lots of free time. Favorite activities included dancing, playing games, and making music—using flutes, pan pipes, and harps.

DID YOU KNOW?
PLAYS WERE USUALLY FREE, SO ANYONE COULD ATTEND. RICH PEOPLE AND POLITICIANS WOULD PAY FOR THE PERFORMANCES TO MAKE THEMSELVES POPULAR WITH THE PUBLIC.

THEATERS

Every Greek town had a theater where plays would be performed. Women were not allowed to act, so all the parts were played by men. They often wore masks to show different moods and feelings. Many famous **playwrights**, including Euripides and Sophocles, came from ancient Greece.

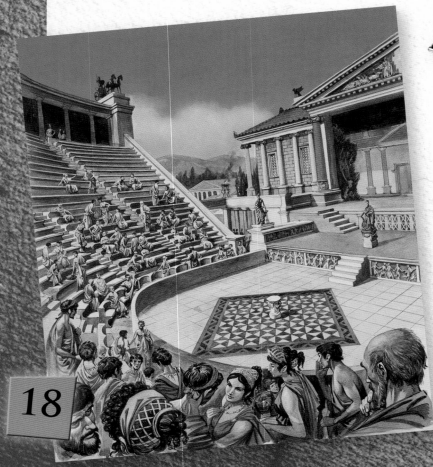

Greek theaters were like modern stadiums, with sloped seating surrounding a semi-circular stage.

MAKE A GREEK THEATER MASK

The ancient Greeks used masks to show what a character was thinking. Some masks had happy faces, while others looked angry.

◀ Comedy masks were shown with smiling faces.

YOU WILL NEED

BALLOON • NEWSPAPER STRIPS
WHITE SCHOOL GLUE • SCISSORS
PAINTBRUSH AND PAINTS
HOLE PUNCH • STRING • PIN

1 Blow up the balloon to head size. Apply newspaper strips and glue to the front of the balloon.

2 Build up several layers of newspaper strips and leave to dry. Pop the balloon and remove it.

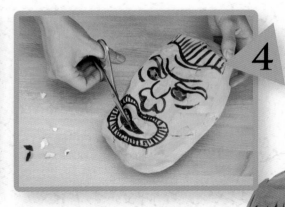

3 Paint the mask and leave it to dry. Then paint an expression—happy, angry, or sad.

4 Carefully cut out holes for the eyes and mouth.

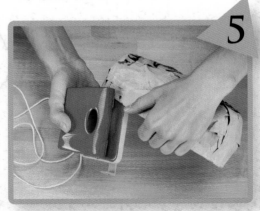

5 Make a hole on each side of the mask. Thread one piece of string through each hole and tie a knot.

Tie the mask to your head. You could make several masks with different expressions and put on a play with your friends. ▶

THE OLYMPIC GAMES

The Greeks put on many different festivals, but the most important were the Olympic Games. They were held every four years in a place called Olympia, in celebration of Zeus. **Athletes** came from all over the Greek world to the games. City-states that were at war would even stop fighting during the games, so athletes could travel safely.

◄ One ancient Greek sport was javelin throwing. This is still performed at the modern Olympic Games.

DIFFERENT SPORTS

At the ancient Olympics, athletes competed in many different sports, including running races, throwing the discus and javelin, wrestling, and boxing. Today, Olympic athletes take part in many of the same sports, as well as new ones, such as cycling, basketball, and tennis. Since 1924, a separate games called the Winter Olympics has also been held.

DID YOU KNOW?
IN ANCIENT GREECE, ALL OF THE ATHLETES COMPETED NAKED AT THE OLYMPIC GAMES.

◄ At the 2004 Olympic Games in Athens, winning athletes were presented with victory wreaths, just like ancient athletes.

THE MODERN OLYMPICS

The first of the ancient Greek Olympic Games were held in 776 BC and the last in AD 393, over a thousand years later in Roman times. In 1896, a Frenchman called Baron Pierre de Coubertin, who was interested in the ancient Olympics, decided to hold the games in Athens. Since then, the modern Olympics have been held every four years in a different city around the world.

MAKE A
VICTORY OLIVE WREATH

Instead of a gold medal, the winners at the ancient Olympics were given a wreath. It was made from olive branches and worn on their heads.

YOU WILL NEED
GREEN PAPER • LIGHT AND DARK GREEN CARDSTOCK
SCISSORS • PENCIL • STAPLER
GLUE

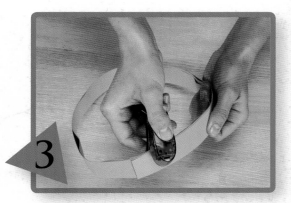

1 Cut out a long strip of green paper, 28 in (70 cm) by 2 in (5 cm).

2 Fold the paper in half lengthwise. Curl the paper into a loop, placing one end inside the other.

3 Place the loop on your head and push the ends past each other until it fits. Staple ends together.

4 Cut out 30 leaf shapes from the cardstock. They should be about 5 in (12 cm) long and 2.5 in (6 cm) wide.

5 Fold the leaves in half and glue the stalks inside the folded edges of the headband.

You could hold a race and give your Olympic wreath to the winner. ▶

21

HOMES, WOMEN, AND CHILDREN

There were many different types of houses in ancient Greece. Poor people lived in small, simple homes. Rich people lived in large houses decorated with mosaics —pictures made out of small, colored pieces of stone. Town houses had a central courtyard or garden. Walls—of mud-brick, stone or wood—were covered in plaster and painted white to keep out the sun's heat.

◄ A mosaic floor from a house on the Greek island of Delos. Only the wealthiest families could afford mosaics.

MAKE A GREEK YO-YO

Ancient pictures have been found showing Greek children playing with yo-yos, which many historians believe were invented in Greece.

 This picture from 500 BC is believed to show a youth playing with a yo-yo.

YOU WILL NEED
MODELING CLAY
MODELING TOOL • PIECE OF
CANE • 3.3 FT (1 M) LENGTH OF
STRING • STANLEY KNIFE

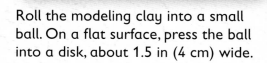

1

Roll the modeling clay into a small ball. On a flat surface, press the ball into a disk, about 1.5 in (4 cm) wide.

4

Ask an adult to cut a hole in the center of each disk. Push the cane through the hole of one disk.

22

WOMEN

In ancient Greece, women did not have many rights. They were not allowed to vote and only a few women were allowed to work. When a woman got married, she had to give everything she owned, including all her money, to her husband. Women had to bring up the children and look after the house.

A woman at work at a table in ancient Greece.

CHILDREN

When a child was born in ancient Greece, the father decided if it lived or died. If the child was sick, or if the family was not wealthy, the child was sometimes left behind, or sold as a slave. Boys were sent to school from the age of seven, but girls stayed at home.

2 Use a modeling tool to carefully cut the large disk into two equal-sized smaller disks, each 0.8 in (2 cm) wide.

3 Ask an adult to cut a cane into a 2 in- (5 cm-) long piece.

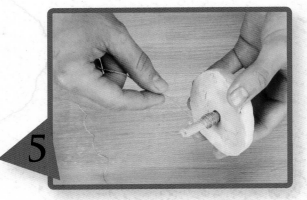

5 Wrap the string around the cane sticking out. Push the other disk onto the cane.

Add a small piece of clay to each end of the cane to keep the disks on. Get yo-yoing!

FARMING AND FOOD

▲
This vase from 500 BC shows farm laborers working in the fields. They are using oxen to pull a plow.

Greece is a hot, dry country with many mountains. It doesn't often rain and much of its soil is poor, making it bad for growing certain crops. This forced many Greeks to move abroad and start new colonies in places such as Italy. When the harvest was bad in Greece, food could be bought from these places to feed people.

FOOD

Most Greek settlements were near the coast, so the Greeks ate a lot of fish. Meat was eaten less often. The Greeks also ate olives, grown throughout the country, honey, olive oil, and bread made from wheat or barley. People also kept goats and chickens to provide milk and eggs.

DID YOU KNOW?
THE GREEKS USUALLY DID THEIR COOKING OUTDOORS SO THAT THE SMELLS DID NOT LINGER WITHIN THE HOUSE.

Olives are grown on trees. They were squeezed to produce olive oil. It was used in cooking and as a fuel for lamps.
▼

An amphora was a large clay pot used to transport and store liquid, especially wine and olive oil.
▼

DRINK

Grapes are one of the few crops that grow well on Greece's dry, sun-baked hills. Grapes were eaten by the ancient Greeks and used to make wine. The Greeks also sent wine in large clay pots to other parts of the Greek world, and traded it with other civilizations.

MAKE A MINI AMPHORA

In ancient Greece, olive oil was transported in large two-handled clay containers called amphorae (*say am-for-ay*).

YOU WILL NEED
MODELING CLAY
PAINTBRUSH AND BROWN
PAINT

1 Take a piece of modeling clay and roll it into a ball about the size of a golf ball.

2 Squeeze the ball into an egg shape. Flatten one of the ends to make a base.

3 Use your finger to make a hole in the other end. Push your finger right down almost to the bottom.

4 Use your fingers to pinch the area around the entrance of the hole into a lip.

5 Roll out two thin sausages of clay. Bend them into C-shapes and attach as arms.

▶ Paint your amphora brown. When it is dry, fill your amphora with the liquid of your choice.

25

CLOTHES AND JEWELRY

This picture shows Aristotle, an ancient Greek philosopher, wearing a chiton and leather sandals.

Most clothes in ancient Greece were made from wool or **linen**. The wealthiest people might have clothes made of silk from China. Most clothes would be colored using dyes from plants, insects, and sea creatures. Poor people's clothes were plain and simple.

WHAT TO WEAR
Both men and women wore similar styles of clothes. The main item of clothing was called a chiton. This was like a long dress, fastened with pins. **Tunics** and cloaks were also worn. People looked at themselves in mirrors made from polished bronze.

DID YOU KNOW?
MOST ANCIENT GREEKS DIDN'T WEAR SHOES. SANDALS, MADE OF LEATHER, WOULD ONLY BE WORN ON SPECIAL OCCASIONS.

HAIR AND JEWELRY
The ancient Greeks were very fashionable. Both men and women took great care of their hair. Men often curled their hair and women wore pins to decorate their hair. Wearing jewelry was also popular. Poor people wore jewelry made from copper, while rich people wore pieces made from gold, silver, and precious stones.

Ancient Greece had many skilled craftsmen who created jewelry, such as these gold earrings.

MAKE A CHITON

A chiton was a simple, loose, flowing garment that kept the Greeks cool on hot summer days.

YOU WILL NEED
SHEET, AROUND 6.5 FT (2 M) X 4.5 FT (1.4 M) • SAFETY PINS
NEEDLE AND THREAD • STRING

1 Fold the sheet in half.

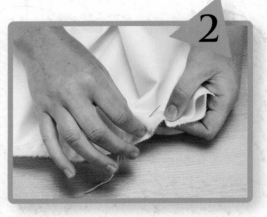

2 Ask an adult to help you to sew together the edges opposite the fold.

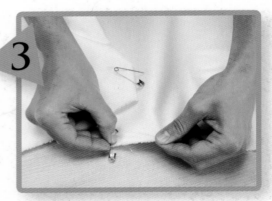

3 Decide which end is going to be the top. Attach safety pins where your shoulders will be, two on each side.

4 Put the chiton on over your head. Use the string to tie the chiton around your waist.

In ancient Greece, working men wore short tunics, which allowed them to move more freely. Women wore long chitons.

The belt is called a *zoster*. It can be worn around the chest or waist.

27

GREAT THINKERS

Ancient Greece was home to some very clever people, who came up with new ideas in mathematics, astronomy, and medicine. These ideas changed the world forever. For example, the astronomer, Aristarchus, was the first person to realize that the Earth travels around the Sun. Pythagoras was a mathematician whose calculations are still used today. Hippocrates was a doctor who developed many ways to help save people's lives.

◄ This modern picture shows Hippocrates, who is often called the "father of modern medicine," performing a medical operation.

MAKE AN ANCIENT GREEK DOOR PLAQUE

The Greek alphabet has been used since the 8th century BC, making it one of the oldest in the world.

Paint the cardstock yellow.

Greek Letter	Modern Letter	Greek Letter	Modern Letter
A α	A	Ν ν	N
Β β	B	Ξ ξ	X
Γ γ	G	Ο ο	O
Δ δ	D	Π π	P
Ε ε	E	Ρ ρ	R
Ζ ζ	Z	Σ σ	S
Η η	H	Τ τ	T
Θ θ	Th	Υ υ	U
Ι ι	I	Φ φ	Ph
Κ κ	K	Χ χ	Ch
Λ λ	L	Ψ ψ	Ps
Μ μ	M	Ω ω	O

DID YOU KNOW?
TODAY, DOCTORS TAKE A MODERN VERSION OF THE HIPPOCRATIC OATH, NAMED AFTER HIPPOCRATES. THEY PROMISE TO PUT THEIR PATIENTS' HEALTH FIRST.

PHILOSOPHERS

The most important thinkers in ancient Greece were called philosophers. Philosophy means the "love of wisdom" and philosophers were often clever in several different subjects, including science, mathematics, and art. Two of the most famous philosophers were Socrates and Plato.

SHIPS AND TRADE

The ancient Greeks made ships that could travel long distances and carry a lot of cargo. This was important because many Greek settlements were on islands. The Greeks also used ships, called **triremes**, to fight. Powered by a team of rowers, one ship would ram fast into another to try to sink it.

▲
Socrates, one of the great Greek philosophers, writes a hymn after he has been sentenced to death.

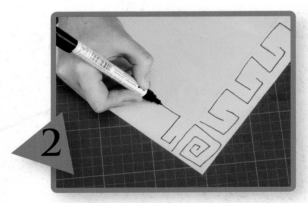

Draw an ancient Greek border around the edge of your tag.

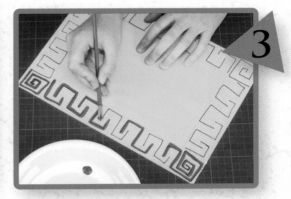

Paint the border using different colors.

Attach your finished piece to your bedroom door.

▼

Using the Greek alphabet, write your name in pencil. Then go over it with marker pen or paint.

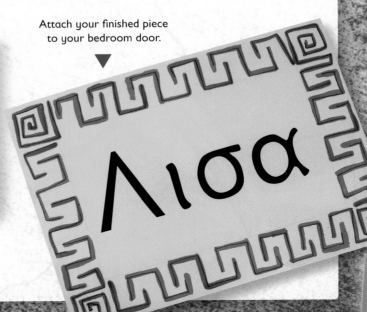

GLOSSARY

Archeologist Someone who studies ancient sites and artifacts.

Athlete Someone who plays sports.

City-state A city and the surrounding area that forms an independent state.

Civilization The way of life and shared culture, art, and architecture of a group of people.

Colony When people from one area or country settle in, or take over another area or country, it is known as a colony.

Democracy Where everyone is equal and can vote.

Empire A group of countries, states, or people controlled by a single ruler, known as the emperor.

Festival A time of mass celebration, usually held at the same time each year.

Free man Male citizen of a Greek city-state who is not a slave.

Fresco A painting made on a wall when the plaster is wet.

Linen A type of cloth that is woven from fibers taken from a plant known as flax.

Persian Empire A large empire that stretched across what is now modern Iran and into Asia.

Philosopher A person who tries to find answers to problems, about truth, justice, and the meaning of life, using carefully thought-out arguments.

Playwright Someone who writes plays.

Prophecy A prediction of future events.

Relief A method of carving that makes the figures stand out from a flat background.

Settlements A place where people live all year round. Cities, towns, and villages are all settlements.

Slave Someone who is owned by another person and works for them for no money.

State A single area or country controlled by a single government or ruler.

Temple Building where people come to worship.

Trading Buying and selling goods.

Trireme An ancient Greek warship, powered by teams of rowers.

Tunic A loose, sleeveless item of clothing, like a long waistcoat.

Tyrant In ancient Greece, tyrants were rulers who governed without asking the people their views.

Worship To show respect and love for a god, especially by praying in a religious building.

INDEX

31

NOTES FOR PARENTS AND TEACHERS

- Read all about the exciting lives and adventures of ancient Greek gods and heroes at www.ancientgreece.com/s/Mythology/ or http://greece.mrdonn.org/myths.html. Get the children to make a family tree of the Greek gods, or to create a picture book retelling their favorite Greek myth.

- Find out the history of the ancient Olympic Games at the official website of the modern Olympics, www.olympic.org/uk/games/ancient/index_uk.asp. Look at ancient art depicting the events, find out which famous Greeks took part (including the philosopher Plato) and read the rather harsh rules of the games—which stated that any athlete found cheating could be whipped. Ancient Olympic winners had poems written in their honor. Ask the children to write their own poem about a modern Olympic hero.

- Play interactive games and take a quiz on ancient Greece at this website for 7–8 year olds, www.mystery-productions.com/hyper/hypermedia_2003/Miller/AM_hypermedia/Artifact/.

- Read a play about the 5th century BC war between the city-states of Athens and Sparta, as seen through the eyes of two families—one Athenian, one Spartan—at this excellent elementary school site: http://home.freeuk.net/elloughton13/greece.htm. Children could write their own play about another episode in Greek history—perhaps the Trojan War, or Alexander's conquests.

- Discover the ancient Greek world beyond Greece. Alexander the Great was one of the most successful military leaders in history. Follow his victorious progress across Europe and Asia in the 4th century BC on the moving map at http://greece.mrdonn.org/alexander.html. Print a map and get the children to mark and name all the significant ancient Greek settlements.

Useful websites

- Follow an ancient Greek timeline at www.bbc.co.uk/schools/ancientgreece/main_menu.shtml.

- Read about the Trojan War and look at artifacts from the museum's collection at www.britishmuseum.org/explore/families_and_children/online_tours/the_trojan_war/the_trojan_war.aspx.

- Take online tours of Greece's major archeological sites with the Hellenic Ministry of Culture at www.culture.gr/war/index_en.jsp.